GEOMETRIC

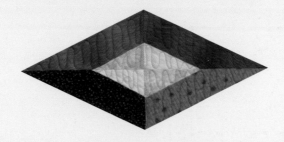

GEMS

GEOMETRIC

Quilts from Diamonds, Circles, and Squares

Cathy Wierzbicki

GEMS

Martingale®
& COMPANY

Geometric Gems: Quilts from Diamonds,
Circles, and Squares
© 2010 by Cathy Wierzbicki

That Patchwork Place® is an imprint of
Martingale & Company®.

Martingale & Company
20205 144th Ave. NE
Woodinville, WA 98072-8478 USA
www.martingale-pub.com

Credits

President & CEO: Tom Wierzbicki
Editor in Chief: Mary V. Green
Managing Editor: Tina Cook
Developmental Editor: Karen Costello Soltys
Technical Editor: Laurie Baker
Copy Editor: Marcy Heffernan
Design Director: Stan Green
Production Manager: Regina Girard
Illustrator: Robin Strobel
Cover & Text Designer: Stan Green
Photographer: Brent Kane

Mission Statement

Dedicated to providing quality products and service
to inspire creativity.

Printed in China
15 14 13 12 11 10   8 7 6 5 4 3 2 1

**Library of Congress Cataloging-in-Publication Data
is available upon request.**

ISBN: 978-1-56477-982-3

I climbed up the door and opened the stairs,

ACKNOWLEDGMENTS

Thank you once again to Bonnie Gibbs, my go-to machine quilter. I'm always excited to see what she adds to my quilts—her work never disappoints. Thank you, also, to Lanae Rohwer of Ankeny, Iowa. She quilted my "Nine Patch with an Attitude" on very short notice, and she did a beautiful job. All of my machine-quilted projects are enhanced because of the talents of these creative ladies, and I am grateful for their contributions.

My sincere thanks and appreciation are also extended to every quilt-shop owner, guild-program chairwoman, quilt-show organizer, and retreat and cruise scheduler who has ever invited me to visit their events. I have thoroughly enjoyed sharing my quilting passion with each of them. I look forward to hearing from more quilters so that we can schedule future sharing opportunities and spend time quilting together.

I turned off the bed and crawled into the light,

All because you kiss me goodnight.

CONTENTS

INTRODUCTION

You're about to discover how easy it is to jazz up your quilts by working with an array of interesting angles. For some of these quilts, you'll also learn that templates and acrylic tools can be your best friends! There was a time I avoided any quilt block that required the use of templates; that is, until I tried them. Suddenly it wasn't as frightening as I'd led myself to believe.

These are totally doable designs, although not all of them can be made in a day or even a weekend. That's OK—the payoff will be eye-catching quilts that you can be proud of. You might even end up with a showstopper or ribbon winner!

Thank you for taking this quilting journey with me, and may you always take time to quilt.

~Cathy

By Cathy Wierzbicki; machine quilted by Bonnie Gibbs

SQUARE DEAL

THIS BOLD AND BRIGHT QUILT IS HIGH ON IMPACT BUT EASY ON CUTTING. A FEW TRIANGLES AND CIRCLES ADD INTEREST, AND THE LARGE OPEN SPACES ARE PERFECT FOR QUILTING YOUR FAVORITE MOTIFS.

Finished quilt size: 57" x 76½"

MATERIALS

Yardage is based on 42"-wide fabric.

1⅝ yards of focus print for large squares, circle appliqués, and outer border
⅝ yard of salmon-colored fabric for filler strips
⅝ yard of assorted prints for small squares
½ yard of lime green fabric for outer border
⅜ yard of white print for sashing
½ yard of turquoise print for filler strips
⅓ yard of red fabric for sashing
⅓ yard of black-and-white print for cornerstones, sashing, and inner border
¼ yard *each* of one dark print and one light print for flying-geese units
¼ yard of yellow fabric for inner border
⅝ yard of fabric for binding
3⅞ yards of fabric for backing
61" x 81" piece of batting
Template-making material

CUTTING

From the dark print for flying-geese units, cut:

3 squares, 6¾" x 6¾"; cut each square twice diagonally to yield 12 triangles (A) (you will use 10)

From the light print for flying-geese units, cut:

10 squares, 3⅝" x 3⅝"; cut each square once diagonally to yield 20 triangles (B)

From the focus print, cut:

2 strips, 12½" x 42"; crosscut into 5 squares, 12½" x 12½" (C)
4 strips, 6" x 42"

From the red fabric, cut:

2 rectangles, 1½" x 12½" (D)
2 strips, 1½" x 38½" (E)
3 strips, 1½" x 42"

From the turquoise print, cut:

2 strips, 6" x 25½" (F)
2 rectangles, 6" x 12½" (G)

From the assorted prints, cut a *total* of:

17 squares, 6" x 6" (H)

From the black-and-white print, cut:

3 strips, 1½" x 42"
2 strips, 1½" x 25½" (I)
7 squares, 1½" x 1½" (J)

From the white print, cut:

7 strips, 1½" x 42"; crosscut into:
   10 rectangles, 1½" x 12½" (K)
   21 rectangles, 1½" x 6" (L)

From the salmon-colored fabric, cut:

3 strips, 6" x 42"

From the lime green fabric, cut:

3 strips, 5" x 42"

From the yellow fabric, cut:

4 strips, 1½" x 42"

From the fabric for binding, cut:

8 strips, 2¼" x 42"

Making the Quilt-Top Sections

1. To make the flying-geese units, sew a B triangle to the short sides of each A triangle. Make 10. Sew two units together along the long edges, with the points facing in the same direction. Make five flying-geese units.

Make 10. Make 5.

2. Using pieces C–F, H, I, and L, assemble section 1.

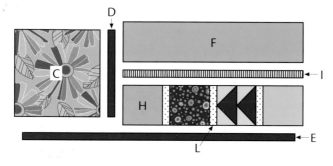

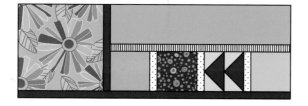

3. Using pieces C, G, H, and J–L, assemble section 2.

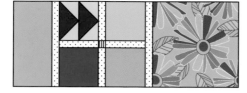

Section 2.
Make 1.

4. Using pieces C, G, H, and J–L, assemble section 3.

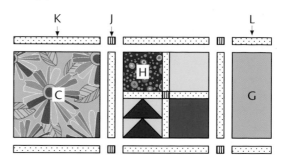

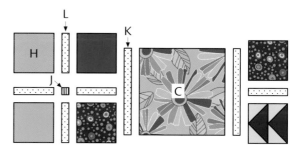

Section 3.
Make 1.

5. Using pieces C, H, and J–L, assemble section 4.

Section 4.
Make 1.

6. With right sides together, join the three red 1½" x 42" strips to make one long strip using diagonal seams. From the pieced strip, cut two strips, 51½" long. Repeat with the three salmon 6" x 42" strips.

7. Sew each red 1½" x 51½" strip to the long edge of the salmon 6" x 51½" strips to make section 5.

Section 5.
Make 2.

ASSEMBLING THE QUILT TOP

1. Refer to the illustration below to sew sections 2, 3, and 4 together along the long edges.

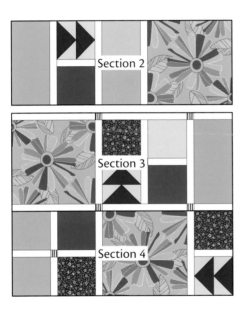

2. Pin a section 1 to the top of section 2, aligning the edges along the right edge. Sew from the right edge to a little more than halfway across section 2; backstitch. Pin the remaining section 1 to the bottom of section 4, aligning the edges along the left edge. Sew from the left edge to a little more than halfway across section 4; backstitch.

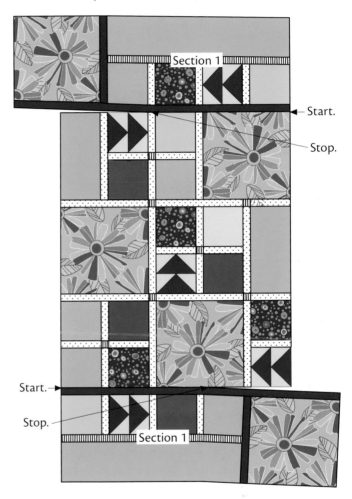

3. Fold back the unsewn end of the top section 1. Sew a section 5 to the left edge of the quilt top, making sure the red strip is closest to the quilt center section. Fold back the unsewn end of the bottom section 1 and sew the remaining section 5 to the right edge of the quilt top in the same manner. Finish sewing the remainder of the top section 1 and the bottom section 1 to the quilt top.

4. Using diagonal seams, sew the three black-and-white 1½" x 42" strips together to make one long strip. Measure the length of the quilt top through the center. From the pieced strip, cut one piece to this length. Sew the strip to the left side of the quilt top. Measure the width of the quilt top through the center. From the remainder of the pieced strip, cut one piece to this length. Sew the strip to the bottom of the quilt top.

5. Sew the three lime green 5" x 42" strips together to make one long strip using diagonal seams. Cut the strip to the same length as the previously sewn black-and-white strip. Sew the strip to the bottom of the quilt top. Measure the length of the quilt top through the center. From the remainder of the pieced strip, cut one piece to this length. Sew the strip to the left side of the quilt top.

6. Repeat step 4 with the four yellow 1½" x 42" strips, adding them to the right edge and then the top edge of the quilt top. Repeat with the focus print 6" x 42" strips, also adding them to the right edge and then the top edge of the quilt top.

7. Refer to "Making and Using Templates" on page 43 to make a template from the template-making material using the circle pattern below. Use the template to cut six circles from the remainder of the focus fabric. Appliqué three circles to each of

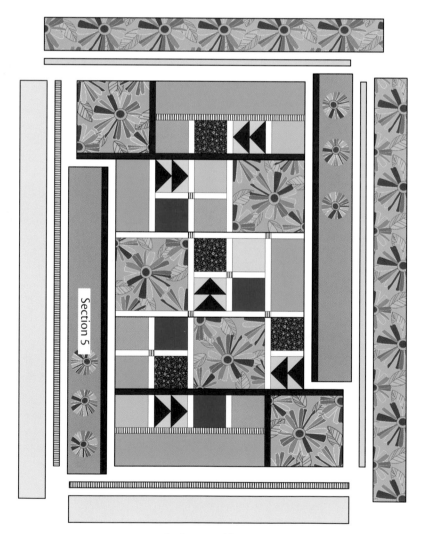

Quilt assembly

the salmon strips using your preferred method and referring to the photo on page 8 as necessary.

FINISHING

1. Layer the quilt top with batting and backing; baste.
2. Quilt as desired.
3. Refer to "Making Painless Mitered Binding" on page 45 to bind the quilt with the binding strips.

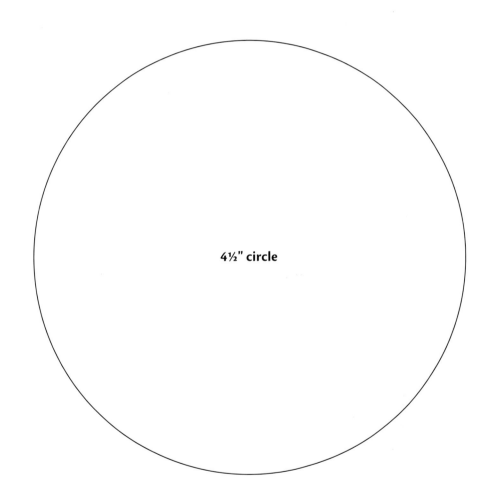

4½" circle

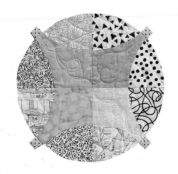

NINE PATCH WITH AN ATTITUDE

GENTLE ARCS ARE EASY TO SEW WITH THE AID OF JUST ONE PIN! THE SECRET IS PLACING THE CORRECT PIECE ON TOP WHEN SEWING THE SEAM. THIS BLOCK IS MORE FORGIVING THAN MANY OTHER CURVED DESIGNS, SO DON'T BE AFRAID TO TRY FOLLOWING A LESS-THAN-STRAIGHT PATH.

Finished quilt size: 60" x 60"
Finished block size: 8" x 8"

MATERIALS

Yardage is based on 42"-wide fabric.

2⅝ yards of focus fabric with black background for blocks, outer border, and binding

1⅓ yards *total* of assorted white-with-black prints for blocks

1¼ yards *total* of assorted lime green fabrics for blocks

1¼ yards of black solid fabric for blocks

⅓ yard of gold print for blocks and inner border

4 yards of fabric for backing

68" x 68" piece of batting

Template-making material or Nine Patch with an Attitude acrylic template set (see "Resources" on page 47)

CUTTING

Before you begin cutting, if you are not using the acrylic template set, refer to "Making and Using Templates" on page 43 to make templates for pieces A and B from template-making material using the patterns on page 17. Be sure to include all of the markings.

From the focus fabric, cut:

6 strips, 4¾" x 42"; from the strips, cut 48 pieces using template A

7 strips, 5½" x 42"

7 strips, 2¼" x 42"

From the gold print, cut:

7 strips, 1¼" x 42"; crosscut 2 strips into 36 squares, 1¼" x 1¼"

From the assorted lime green fabrics, cut a *total* of:

8 strips, 4¾" x 42"; from the strips, cut 52 pieces using template A

From the assorted white-with-black prints, cut a *total* of:

9 strips, 4½" x 42"; from the strips, cut 120 pieces using template B

From the black solid fabric, cut:

6 strips, 4¾" x 42"; from the strips, cut 44 pieces using template A

2 strips, 4½" x 42"; from the strips, cut 24 pieces using template B

MAKING THE BLOCKS

1. Sew two lime green A pieces to opposite sides of a gold print square. Press the seam allowances toward the square. Repeat to make a total of 16 units.

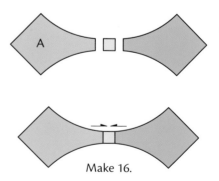

Make 16.

By Cathy Wierzbicki; machine quilted by Lanae Rohwer

2. Lay out a focus fabric A piece between two white-with-black B pieces. *With the A piece on top,* position the A piece over the left B piece. Place a pin at the *end* of the seam (where indicated by the dot) and finger-align the beginning of the seam. Sew a few stitches in the direction of the arrow, and then stop with the needle in the down position. Realign the pieces to keep the raw edges even and continue sewing a few stitches at a time until the entire seam is sewn. Remove the pin as you approach the end of the seam. Repeat to add the right B piece to the A piece, paying attention to the pin placement and sewing direction. Press the seam allowances toward the B pieces. Repeat to make a total of 32 units.

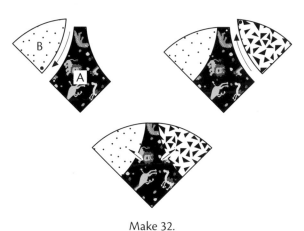

Make 32.

3. With the unit from step 1 on top, sew two units from step 2 to a unit from step 1 to complete the block, aligning the seams and inserting a pin at each intersection and at the end of the seam. Press the seam allowances toward the units from step 2. Repeat to make a total of 16 blocks.

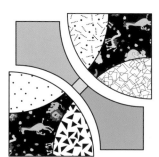

Make 16.

4. Repeat steps 1–3 with the remaining A and B pieces to make blocks in the following arrangements.

Make 8.   Make 8.   Make 4.

Assembling the Quilt Top

1. Refer to the quilt assembly diagram below to arrange the blocks in six rows of six blocks each. Make sure the blocks with the black solid A pieces are placed around the perimeter and rotate the blocks as necessary to achieve the design.

2. Sew the remainder of the gold print 1¼"-wide strips together end to end using diagonal seams. From the pieced strip, cut four strips 62" long. Repeat with the focus fabric 5½"-wide strips.

3. Sew each gold print strip to a focus print strip along one long edge. Make four border strips.

Make 4.

4. Refer to "Borders with Mitered Corners" on page 44 to sew the borders to the quilt top.

Quilt assembly

FINISHING

1. Layer the quilt top with batting and backing; baste.
2. Quilt as desired.
3. Refer to "Making Painless Mitered Binding" on page 45 to bind the quilt with the focus fabric 2¼"-wide strips.

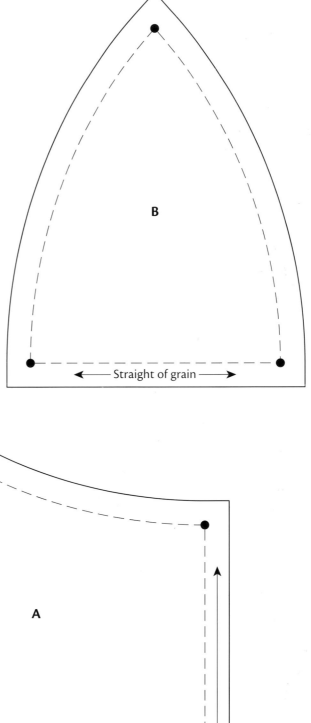

B

← Straight of grain →

A

¼" seam allowance

THINK INSIDE THE BOX

THESE 60° DIAMONDS COME TOGETHER IN VERTICAL ROWS, MAKING STACKED CUBES THAT APPEAR THREE-DIMENSIONAL. I "FILLED" MY BOXES WITH THINGS LITTLE BOYS MIGHT COLLECT—ROCKS, SHELLS, BUGS, AND MORE. WHAT WILL YOU PUT IN YOUR BOXES?

Finished quilt size: 44" x 51½"

MATERIALS

Yardage is based on 42"-wide fabric.

1½ yards of medium-dark fabric for background and border

3" x 13" strip *each* of 23 assorted focus fabrics for box interiors*

1¼" x 22" strip *each* of 23 assorted light fabrics, 23 assorted medium fabrics, and 23 assorted dark fabrics. Each fabric should coordinate with one of the focus fabrics. The light, medium, and dark fabrics for each focus fabric should be from the same color family.*

½ yard of gold print for binding

3 yards of fabric for backing

52" x 60" piece of batting

Template-making material or Think Inside the Box acrylic template (see "Resources" on page 47)

*Each strip is enough for one "box." Use the same fabric more than once if desired.

CUTTING

From the medium-dark fabric, cut:

1 strip, 4¾" x 42"; crosscut into 4 rectangles, 4¾" x 8"

5 strips, 4½" x 42"

6 strips, 3½" x 42"

From the gold print, cut:

6 strip, 2¼" x 42"

MAKING THE PIECED TRIANGLES

1. If you are not using the acrylic template, refer to "Making and Using Templates" on page 43 to make template A from template-making material using the pattern on page 21. Be sure to include all of the markings.

2. Place the template on a strip of focus fabric so that the tip of the template is aligned with one long edge of the strip and the 3" line on the template is aligned with the opposite long edge. Cut along both sides of the template. Invert the template and cut another triangle. Continue cutting across the strip in this manner until you have cut six triangles. Repeat with the remaining strips of focus fabric. Keep the triangles from each strip together.

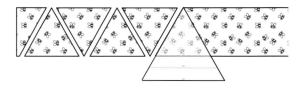

3. Select a light, medium, and dark 1¼" x 22" strip for one set of focus fabric triangles. With right sides together, align one edge of two triangles with the top of the light strip, leaving approximately 1½" between triangles. Sew the

By Cathy Wierzbicki; machine quilted by Bonnie Gibbs

triangles to the strip. Repeat with the medium and dark strips. Press the seam allowances toward the triangles. Position the template on each of the pieced triangles, aligning the 3¾" line of the template with the bottom of the strips. Trim along both edges of the triangles.

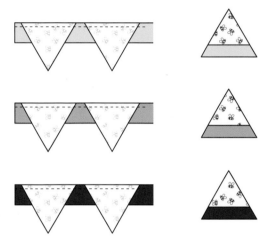

4. With right sides together, sew the pieced triangles with the light strips to the remainder of the light strip as shown, again leaving approximately 1½" between triangles. Repeat with the medium and dark pieced triangles. Press the seam allowances toward the strips. Position the template on each pieced triangle, aligning the bottom of the template with the bottom of the pieced triangle. Trim along both edges.

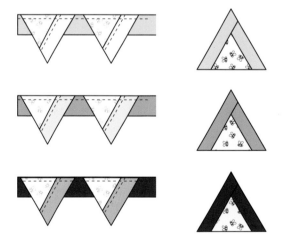

5. Repeat steps 3 and 4 with each of the remaining sets of triangles.

ASSEMBLING THE QUILT TOP

1. Referring to step 2 of "Making the Pieced Triangles," cut 56 triangles from the medium-dark 4½" x 42" strips using the entire template.

2. Arrange the background triangles and pieced triangles for the first long vertical row of five boxes, referring to the quilt assembly diagram on page 21 and the photo on page 19 as needed. Once you have the pieces arranged, separate the row in half vertically. Sew the triangles in each half together into pairs first, and then sew the pairs together. Sew the halves together, carefully matching seam lines. Repeat to make a total of three long vertical rows.

3. Trim the background triangles at the top and bottom of each long vertical row ¼" from the point of the box.

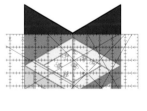

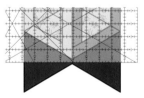

4. Arrange the background triangles and pieced triangles for the first short vertical row of four boxes, referring to the quilt assembly diagram on page 21 and the photo on page 19 as needed.

Sew the pieces together in the same manner as the long vertical rows, and trim the background triangles at the top and bottom of the strip as before. Sew background 4¾" x 8" rectangles to the top and bottom of the strip. Repeat to make a total of two short vertical rows.

5. Refer to the quilt assembly diagram to arrange the long and short vertical rows. Sew the rows together.

6. Refer to "Borders with Butted Corners" on page 44 to sew the medium-dark 3½"-wide borders to the quilt top, piecing the strips as necessary to achieve the correct lengths.

Quilt assembly

FINISHING

1. Layer the quilt top with batting and backing; baste.

2. Quilt as desired.

3. Refer to "Making Painless Mitered Binding" on page 45 to bind the quilt with the focus fabric 2¼"-wide strips.

3"

3¾"

4½"

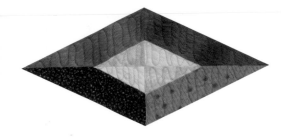

DIAMOND DUST

THIS QUILT WAS DESIGNED FOR 2½" STRIPS OF FABRIC. I GIVE INSTRUCTIONS HERE FOR CUTTING YOUR OWN, BUT YOU COULD EASILY USE A PRECUT ASSORTMENT. SEPARATE THE STRIPS INTO LIGHTS AND DARKS, AND THEN SEW THEM INTO STRIP SETS. YOU'LL BE DAZZLING YOURSELF WITH BEAUTIFUL DIAMONDS IN NO TIME AT ALL.

Finished quilt size: 64½" x 80½"
Finished block size: 8" x 16"

MATERIALS

Yardage is based on 42"-wide fabric.
5 yards *total* of assorted light fabrics
5 yards *total* of assorted dark or medium fabrics
1 yard of accent or contrast fabric
2 yard of fabric for binding
5 yards of fabric for backing
69" x 85" piece of batting
See-through template plastic

CUTTING

From the assorted light fabrics, cut a *total* of:
66 strips, 2½" x 42"

From the assorted dark or medium fabric, cut a *total* of:
66 strips, 2½" x 42"

From the accent or contrast fabric, cut:
12 strips, 2½" x 42"

From the fabric for binding, cut:
8 strips, 2¼" x 42"

MAKING THE DIAMOND BLOCKS

1. Refer to "Making and Using Templates" on page 43 to make templates for the large and small rectangles using the patterns on pages 25 and 26. Be sure to include all of the markings. You will be using both sides of these templates to cut your blocks, so flip each template over and mark the reverse side with an R.

2. Alternately join two light strips and two dark or medium strips along the long edges to make a strip set. Repeat to make a total of 24 strips sets.

3. Position the large rectangle template on a strip set so that the markings on the template correspond with the fabrics and seam lines. Carefully cut around the perimeter of the template with a rotary cutter. (If you're uncomfortable using the rotary cutter along the edge of the template plastic, trace around the plastic with a sharp pencil or fabric marker, remove the template, and then use your ruler and rotary cutter to cut on the marked lines.) Cut two rectangles in one direction; then turn the template to the reverse side and cut two more rectangles, making sure the markings correspond with the fabrics. Repeat with the remaining strip sets. Each strip set will yield two right-slanting and two left-slanting units—enough to make one Diamond block. Save your large scraps to use later when cutting the border units.

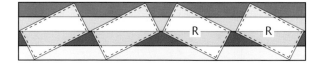

Make 24 strip sets.
Cut 2 left-slanting and 2 right-slanting
rectangles from each strip set.

Cut 48.   Cut 48.

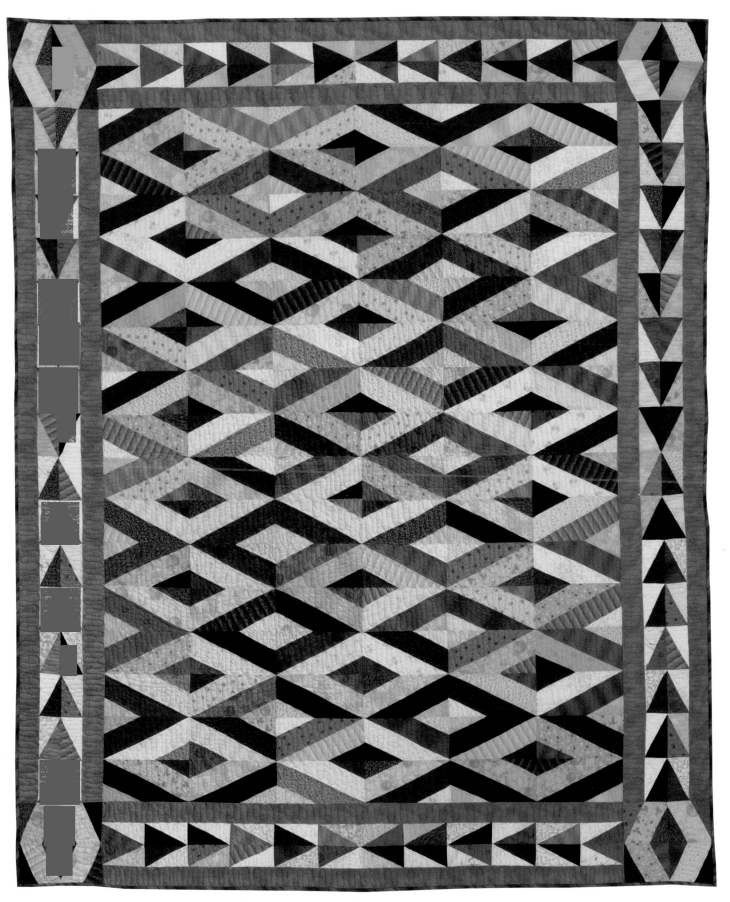

By Cathy Wierzbicki; machine quilted by Bonnie Gibbs

4. Sew four different rectangles from step 3 together. Repeat to make a total of 24 Diamond blocks.

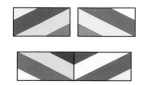

Make 24.

MAKING THE BORDER STRIPS

1. Sew together one light strip and one dark or medium strip along the long edges to make a strip set. Repeat to make a total of 15 strip sets. You will have strips left over to make more strip sets if needed. The actual quantity of strip sets needed will depend on how many units you can cut from the leftovers of the Diamond blocks.

2. Position the small rectangle template on a strip set so that the markings on the template correspond with the fabrics and seam lines. Using the same cutting method as for the Diamond blocks, cut out four left-slanting rectangles, and then reverse the template and cut out four right-slanting rectangles. Cut a total of 72 left-slanting rectangles and 72 right-slanting rectangles using the remaining strip sets and the leftover pieces from the Diamond block strip sets. Make more strip sets if needed to yield the required amount.

Make 15 to 18 strip sets.
Cut a total of 72 left-slanting and
72 right-slanting rectangles.

Cut 72.   Cut 72.

3. Sew a left-slanting and a different right-slanting rectangle from step 2 together to make a pieced triangle. Make a total of 56 pieced triangles.

Make 56.

4. Sew together 12 pieced triangles each for the top and bottom borders, reversing the direction of the triangles at the midpoint of the strip so that all of the points are facing toward the strip center. In the same manner, sew together 16 triangles each for the side borders. Join the accent or contrast 2½" x 42" strips end to end using a diagonal seam. From the pieced strip, cut four strips, 2½" x 48½", and four strips, 2½" x 64½". Sew the 48½"-long strips to the long sides of the top and bottom borders and the 64½"-long strips to the long sides of the side borders.

Top/bottom border.
Make 2.

Side border.
Make 2.

5. From the remaining rectangles from step 2, join four left-slanting rectangles and four right-slanting rectangles to make a corner unit. Repeat to make a total of four units. Sew a unit to each end of the top and bottom borders. Note: I made the corner units for the photographed quilt a different way. This method is easier and slightly more scrappy.

Make 4.

ASSEMBLING THE QUILT TOP

1. Refer to the quilt assembly diagram on page 25 to arrange the Diamond blocks into eight rows of three blocks each. Rearrange the blocks if necessary until you are pleased with the position of the fabrics and colors. Sew the blocks in each row together, and then sew the rows together.

2. Sew the side borders to the quilt top. Join the top and bottom borders to the quilt top.

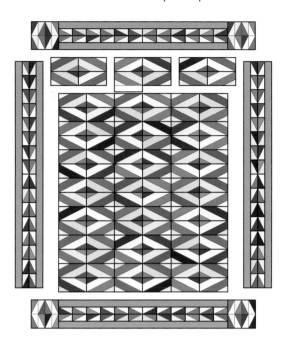

FINISHING

1. Layer the quilt top with batting and backing; baste.
2. Quilt as desired.
3. Refer to "Making Painless Mitered Binding" on page 45 to bind the quilt with the 2¼"-wide binding strips.

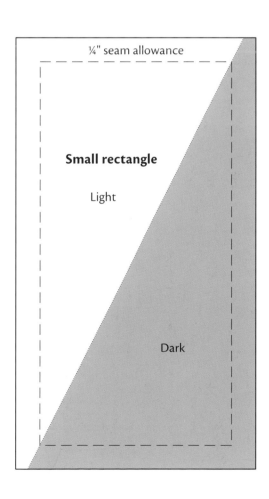

¼" seam allowance

Small rectangle

Light

Dark

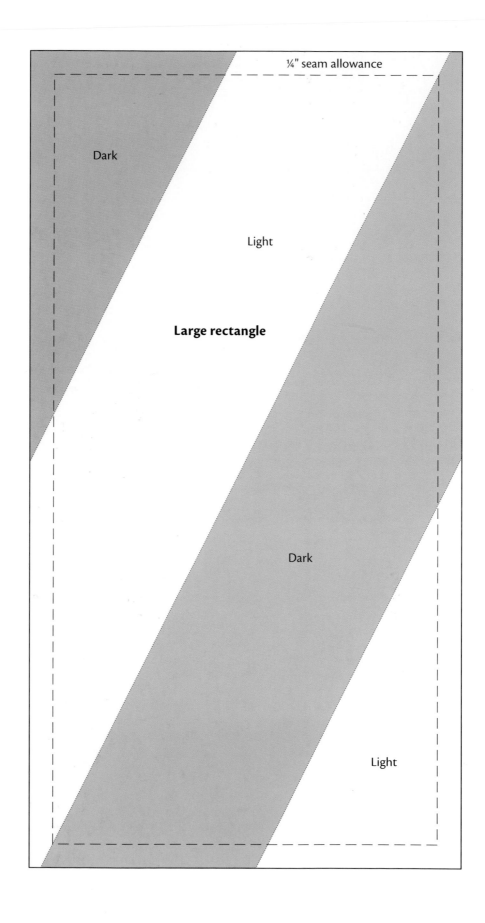

PINEAPPLE NINE PATCH

THE BLOCKS IN THIS QUILT MASQUERADE AS THE CLASSIC PINEAPPLE BLOCK BUT ARE PIECED TOGETHER IN NINE-PATCH FASHION. WHETHER YOU USE SCRAPS OR A PLANNED ASSORTMENT OF FABRICS, YOU'LL BE DELIGHTED AT HOW QUICKLY YOUR QUILT COMES TOGETHER.

Finished quilt size: 84" x 97½"
Finished block size: 13½" x 13½"

MATERIALS

Yardage is based on 42"-wide fabric.

6 yards *total* of assorted dark fabrics (I recommend ½ yard *each* of 12 fabrics) for blocks and borders

5½ yards *total* of assorted light fabrics (I recommend ½ yard *each* of 11 fabrics) for blocks and borders

¾ yard of fabric for binding

8 yards of fabric for backing

92" x 106" piece of batting

See-through template plastic or Tri-Recs™ Tools (available at quilt and fabric shops)

CUTTING

Before you begin cutting, if you are not using the Tri-Recs Tools, refer to "Making and Using Templates" on page 43 to make templates for the A–D pieces using the patterns on page 31. Be sure to include all of the markings. You will be using both sides of these templates to cut your block pieces, so flip each template over and mark the reverse side with an R. To make the best use of your strips when cutting the pieces, invert the template every other cut.

If you are using the Tri-Recs Tools, match the patterns on page 31 with the tool to find the corresponding letter for each piece.

From the assorted dark fabrics, cut a *total* of:

12 strips, 6" x 42"; from the strips, cut 120 pieces using template A

6 strips, 6¾" x 42"; crosscut into 30 squares, 6¾" x 6¾". Cut each square in half twice diagonally to yield 120 triangles (E).

32 strips, 2½" x 42"; from 7 of the strips, cut 168 pieces using template C. Set aside the remaining 25 strips.

From the assorted light fabrics, cut a *total* of:

12 strips, 6" x 42"; from the strips, cut*:
   120 pieces using template B
   120 pieces using template B reversed

15 strips, 2½" x 42"; from the strips, cut*:
   168 pieces using template D
   168 pieces using template D reversed
   22 rectangles, 2½" x 10"

44 strips, 1½" x 42"

From the fabric for binding, cut:

10 strips, 2¼" x 42"

*If you cut from folded strips, each cut will yield 1 regular piece and 1 reversed piece.

MAKING THE BLOCKS

1. Sew one B piece and one B reversed piece to each A piece. The units should measure 6" square.

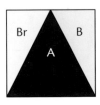

Make 120.

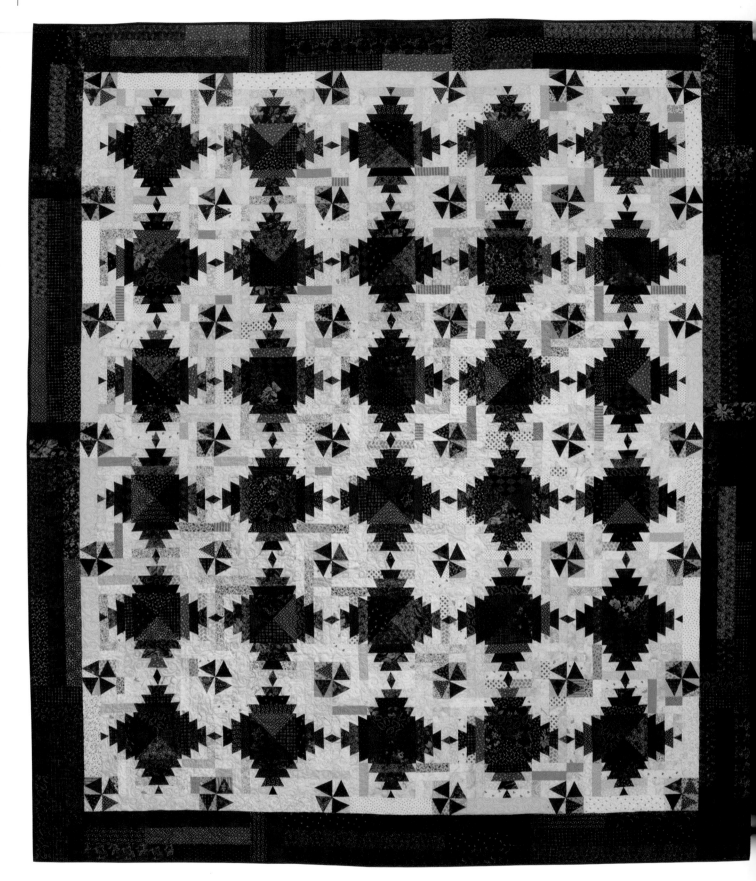

By Cathy Wierzbicki; machine quilted by Bonnie Gibbs

2. Cut each unit horizontally into four 1½"-wide slices. Invert each slice, and then separate the slices from all of the units into stacks of like pieces.

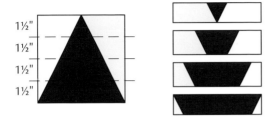

3. Sew the slices back together in their inverted positions to make unit 1, selecting one piece from each stack. Choose four different fabrics for each unit.

Unit 1.
Make 120.

4. To make unit 2, sew one D piece and one D reversed piece to each of the C pieces. The units should measure 2½" square.

Make 168.

5. Sew two assorted light 1½" x 42" strips together along the long edges to make a strip set. Repeat to make a total of 22 strip sets. Crosscut the strip sets into 120 segments 2½" long, and 120 segments 4½" long.

2½"   4½"

Make 22 strip sets.
Cut 120 segments of each width.

6. Sew a 2½"-long segment to the triangle point side of 120 units from step 4. Add a 4½"-long segment to the upper long edge of each of these units. Make sure the dark triangle is always oriented in the same direction. Make a total of 120 units. These units should measure 4½" square. Set aside the remaining units from step 4 for the border.

Unit 2.
Make 120.

7. To make unit 3, select four assorted E triangles. Sew the triangles into pairs, and then sew the pairs together. Repeat to make a total of 30 units.

Unit 3.
Make 30.

8. Select and arrange four *each* of units 1 and 2 and one unit 3 into three horizontal rows. Sew the units in each row together, and then sew the rows together. Repeat to make a total of 30 blocks. The blocks should measure 14" square.

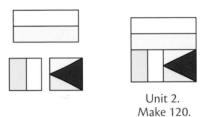 

Make 30.

29

ASSEMBLING THE QUILT TOP

1. Refer to the quilt assembly diagram to lay out the blocks in six rows of five blocks each. Sew the blocks in each row together, and then sew the rows together.

2. Sew C/D units to the ends of a light 2½" x 10" rectangle, orienting the triangles as shown. Repeat to make a total of 22 units.

Make 22.

3. Sew together five units from step 2 to make the top inner-border section. Repeat to make the bottom inner-border section. Refer to the assembly diagram to sew these border strips to the top and bottom of the quilt top, making sure the triangles are oriented correctly. Sew together six units from step 2. Add one of the remaining C/D units to each end of the strip. Repeat to make a total of two side inner borders. Add the borders to the sides of the quilt top.

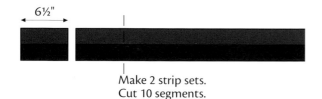

Top/bottom border.
Make 2.

Side border.
Make 2.

4. To make the pieced outer border, sew two different dark 2½" x 42" strips together along the long edges to make a strip set. Repeat to make a total of two strip sets. Crosscut the strip sets into 10 segments, 6½" wide.

6½"

Make 2 strip sets.
Cut 10 segments.

5. Cut the remaining dark 2½" x 42" strips into random lengths between 5" and 22" long. For each strip set, you will need three pieces that are at least 22" long. Sew pieces together end to end with a straight seam to achieve the needed length. Make a total of 42 strips, 22" long. Sew

three strips together along the long edges to make a strip set. Repeat to make a total of 14 strip sets. Trim eight strip sets to 18¾" and the remaining six strip sets to 21¾".

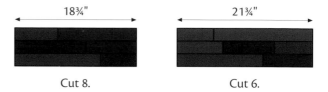

18¾"   21¾"

Cut 8.   Cut 6.

6. Alternately sew together two 6½" segments from step 4 and three 21¾" segments from step 5. Trim 3" from each end of the strip. Repeat to make a total of two borders. Sew these borders to the top and bottom edges of the quilt top. Alternately sew together three 6½" segments and four 18¾" segments. Repeat to make a total of two borders. Sew these borders to the sides of the quilt top.

Quilt assembly

FINISHING

1. Layer the quilt top with batting and backing; baste.

2. Quilt as desired.

3. Refer to "Making Painless Mitered Binding" on page 45 to bind the quilt with the 2¼"-wide binding strips.

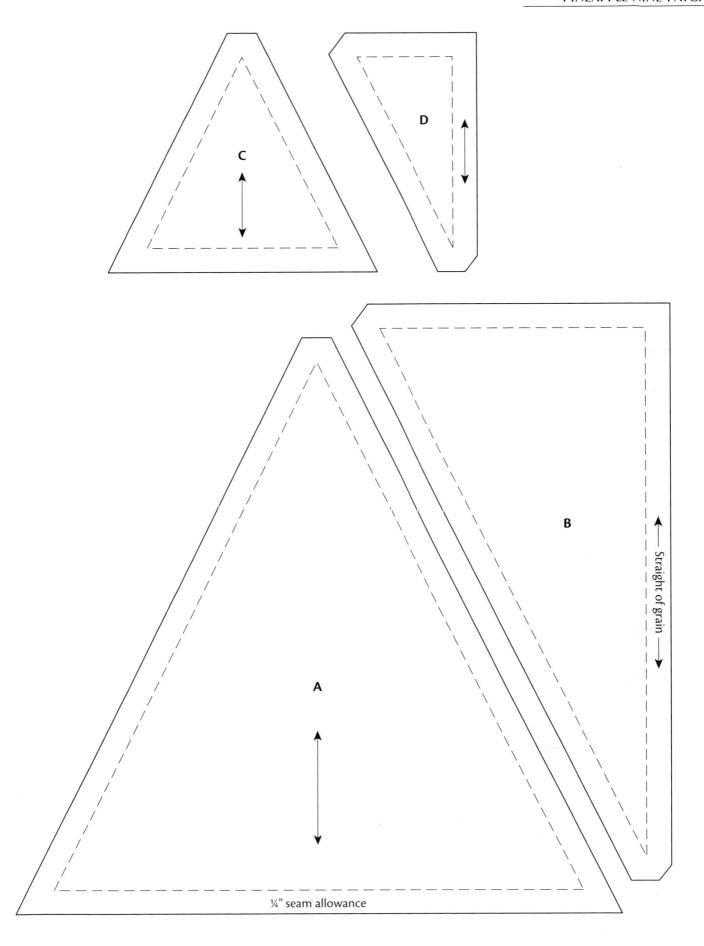

C

D

B

Straight of grain

A

¼" seam allowance

THE LAST WORD

THE SECONDARY PINWHEEL DESIGN IS JUST ONE OF THE THINGS I LIKE ABOUT THIS QUILT. IT'S ALSO A PERSONAL FAVORITE BECAUSE IT GOES TOGETHER QUICKLY AND IS VISUALLY INTERESTING—AND IT ALL HAPPENS WITH A FAIRLY SIMPLE BLOCK.

Finished quilt size: 53½" x 73½"
Finished block size: 10" x 10"

MATERIALS

Yardage is based on 42"-wide fabric.

3⅛ yards of focus fabric for blocks, outer border, and binding

¾ yard of medium green print for blocks

⅝ yard of light gold print 1 for blocks

½ yard of medium rust print for blocks

½ yard of dark brown print for blocks

½ yard of light brown print for blocks

⅓ yard of light gold print 2 for inner border

¼ yard of light fabric for sentiments*

3½ yards of fabric for backing

62" x 82" piece of batting

I used "Comforts of Psalms" preprinted fabric panel from Block Party Studios (see "Resources" on page 47). You could use a plain light fabric and write or stitch you own custom sentiments or use the strips for signatures.

CUTTING

From the light gold print 1, cut:

12 strips, 1½" x 42"; crosscut into 48 rectangles, 1½" x 9½"

From the light fabric for sentiments, cut:

2 strips, 3½" x 42"; crosscut into 8 rectangles, 3½" x 9½", OR fussy cut the rectangles if you are using a preprinted fabric

From the medium rust print, cut:

4 strips, 3½" x 42"; crosscut into 16 rectangles, 3½" x 9½"

From *each* of the dark brown and light brown prints, cut:

2 strips, 4⅜" x 42"; crosscut into 12 squares, 4⅜" x 4⅜". Cut each square in half diagonally to yield 24 triangles (48 total).

1 strip, 4" x 42"; crosscut into 10 squares, 4" x 4" (20 total)

From the focus fabric, cut:

3 strips, 7⅝" x 42"; crosscut the strips into 12 squares, 7⅝" x 7⅝". Cut each square in half twice diagonally to yield 48 triangles.

8 strips, 2¼" x 42"

From the *lengthwise grain* of the remaining focus fabric, cut:

14 rectangles, 6" x 20½"

From the medium green print, cut:

3 strips, 7⅝" x 42"; crosscut the strips into 12 squares, 7⅝" x 7⅝". Cut each square in half twice diagonally to yield 48 triangles.

From light gold print 2, cut:

6 strips, 1½" x 42"; crosscut into 14 rectangles, 1½" x 20½"

By Cathy Wierzbicki; machine quilted by Bonnie Gibbs

MAKING THE BLOCKS

1. Sew light gold 1 rectangles to both long edges of each light fabric rectangle and each rust print rectangle. Add a light brown triangle to the left end of each unit and a dark brown triangle to the right end of each unit.

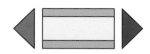

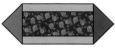

Make 8.   Make 16.

2. Join each focus fabric triangle to a medium green triangle along the short edges.

Make 48.

3. Sew the joined triangles from step 2 to the top and bottom edges of each unit from step 1 to complete the blocks. If you're adding your own sentiments to the blocks, embroider or write them on the light strip of each A block at this time.

Block A.   Block B.
Make 8.   Make 16.

ASSEMBLING THE QUILT TOP

1. Refer to the quilt assembly diagram on page 35 to arrange the blocks in six rows of four blocks each, rotating the blocks to create the pattern. Sew the blocks in each row together, and then sew the rows together.

2. To make the border units, sew each gold print 2 rectangle to a focus fabric rectangle along one long edge. For six of these units, position a dark brown square on the upper-right corner and a light brown square on the upper-left corner; sew diagonally across the square from corner to corner in the direction indicated. Trim ¼" from the stitching lines. Press the triangles toward the upper corners. On four of the remaining units position a dark brown square in the upper-right corner; sew, trim, and press as before. Repeat on the upper-left corner of the remaining four units with the light brown squares.

Make 6.

Make 4.   Make 4.

3. Sew the border units together as shown to make the border strips.

Top/bottom border.
Make 2.

Side border.
Make 2.

4. Refer to "Borders with Mitered Corners" on page 44 to sew the borders to the quilt top.

FINISHING

1. Layer the quilt top with batting and backing; baste.

2. Quilt as desired.

3. Refer to "Making Painless Mitered Binding" on page 45 to bind the quilt with the focus fabric 2¼"-wide binding strips.

Quilt assembly

PAJAMA PRAYER

This large scrap quilt is enhanced with a verse from the song, "I Said My Pajamas," music by George Wyle, lyrics by Edward Pola. It was written in 1949 and recorded by several singers in the 1950s. This charming little verse makes me smile, and I hope it does the same for you. You don't need an expensive embroidery machine to "write" the text; just follow the easy set-up steps to make your own free-motion lettering.

Finished quilt size: 66½" x 84½"

MATERIALS

Yardage is based on 42"-wide fabric.

4½ yards *total* of assorted prints and solid fabrics OR 15 assorted ⅓-yard cuts for pieced blocks and binding

2¼ yards of fabric for border

¾ yard of light solid fabric for text blocks

5¼ yards of fabric for backing

75" x 93" piece of batting

30- or 40-weight rayon or polyester machine-embroidery thread

60-weight bobbin thread

Heat- or water-soluble transparent stabilizer

Tear-away stabilizer

Free-motion embroidery foot or darning foot

90/14 embroidery or topstitch needle

Pen or permanent marker

Masking tape

All-in-One ruler™ (optional)

CUTTING

Refer to the illustrations on pages 39 and 40 as you make your fabric choices for units A–D and be careful that pieces that lie next to each other do not repeat the same fabric. For ease in piecing, label the pieces with the unit and letter as you cut them.

From the light solid fabric for text units, cut:

4 squares, 11" x 11"

From the transparent stabilizer, cut:

4 squares, 11" x 11"

From the tear-away stabilizer, cut:

4 squares, 10½" x 10½"

From the assorted prints and solid fabrics, cut a *total* of:

For unit A:

36 squares, 2" x 2" (A)

36 sets, with each set cut from the same fabric and consisting of:

    2 squares, 2" x 2" (B) (72 total)

    2 rectangles, 2" x 5" (C) (72 total)

For unit B:

18 rectangles, 2" x 6½" (D)

18 sets, with each set cut from the same fabric and consisting of:

    2 rectangles, 2" x 6½" (E) (36 total)

    2 rectangles, 2" x 5" (F) (36 total)

For unit C:

18 squares, 3½" x 3½" (G)

18 sets, with each set cut from the same fabric and consisting of:

    2 rectangles, 2" x 3½" (H) (36 total)

    2 rectangles, 2" x 6½" (I) (36 total)

18 sets, with each set cut from the same fabric and consisting of:

    2 rectangles, 2" x 6½" (J) (36 total)

    2 rectangles, 2" x 9½" (K) (36 total)

By Cathy Wierzbicki; machine quilted by Bonnie Gibbs

For unit D:

4 rectangles, 3½" x 12½" (L)

4 sets, with each set cut from the same fabric and consisting of:

> 2 rectangles, 2" x 12½" (M) (8 total)
>
> 2 rectangles, 2" x 6½" (N) (8 total)

4 sets, with each set cut from the same fabric and consisting of:

> 2 rectangles, 2" x 15½" (O) (8 total)
>
> 2 rectangles, 2" x 9½" (P) (8 total)

For binding:

Random lengths of 2¼"-wide strips to equal approximately 330" when pieced together end to end using diagonal seams

From the *lengthwise grain* of the fabric for border, cut:

2 strips, 6½" x 72½"

2 strips, 6½" x 66½"

STITCHING THE TEXT UNITS

Many quilters use their sewing machines to write words or phrases as they machine quilt, or to create quilt labels. If you simply rotate your sewing machine at a 45° angle and use a zigzag stitch, you can create extraordinary free-motion lettering that looks like embroidery. Here's how to do it.

1. Set your sewing machine on a tabletop and establish a 45° angle. My preferred way to do this is with the All-in-One Ruler. Place the angled edge of the ruler along the front edge of the tabletop and tape the ruler in place with masking tape. Align the front edge of your sewing machine with the edge of the ruler. (Another option is to fold any square in half diagonally and align your machine with that 45° angle.) Position yourself directly in front of the needle—the machine is rotated, but your seating position is not.

2. Install the free-motion embroidery foot on your machine and make sure you are using the standard slotted throat plate, not the single-hole throat plate. Insert the 90/14 needle and thread the top with embroidery thread and the bobbin with bobbin thread. Lower the feed dogs.

3. Set the zigzag stitch width to a wide setting—4.0 to 5.0 is a good place to start—adjusting the width depending on your machine and the desired appearance of your letters. Set the top thread tension at 1, and then experiment to find the optimum setting, adjusting the tension up or down as necessary. You'll know you have the proper setting when the stitches lie flat and even, the fabric does not "tunnel," and none of the bobbin thread is visible on top of the fabric.

4. Enlarge the verse patterns on page 42 by 250%. Position each of the transparent stabilizer squares on top of an enlarged text pattern and trace the words onto the square using a pen or permanent marker.

5. Follow the manufacturer's instructions to apply the tear-away stabilizer to the wrong side of the text fabric square. Pin a transparent stabilizer square to the top of each square.

6. Place a layered fabric square under the machine needle and lower the presser foot. Bring up the bobbin thread at the spot where you want to begin sewing and hold onto both the top and bobbin threads as you begin. Lock your stitches by either sewing in place or beginning with very small stitches; clip the top and bobbin threads at the beginning of the stitching. Sew along the lines of each letter. As you sew, your tendency will be to rotate or twist the fabric you're sewing on. This is exactly what *not* to do. Instead, *slide* the fabric *while always keeping characters parallel to the front edge of the tabletop.* The motion is very much like free-motion quilting. Sew with a fast needle speed, but move the fabric very slowly while stitching over the traced characters. The

result will be satin-stitched letters with no gaps between the threads. Lock your stitches to secure the thread at the beginning and end of each character or word. Remove the stabilizers, press the unit, and trim it to 9½" x 9½". Repeat for the remaining three units.

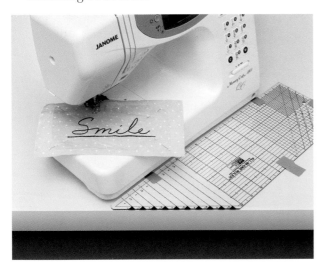

ON-LINE STITCHING

Whenever possible, sew letters in a continuous line. However, some letters (like lowercase *f* and *t*, as well as uppercase *A*, *E*, *K*, and *H*, to name a few) must be stitched in multiple steps. To stitch these letters, you can change to a straight stitch to "travel" along the character, and then resume a zigzag stitch to complete the letter, or you can backstitch rather than stopping and restarting.

MAKING THE PIECED BLOCKS

Press seam allowances away from the center as you add each piece.

1. To make the A units, select an A square and a set of B and C pieces that were cut from a fabric different than the A square fabric. Sew the B squares to opposite sides of the A square. Sew the C rectangles to the top and bottom of the A/B unit. Repeat to make a total of 36 units.

Unit A.
Make 36.

2. To make the B units, select a D rectangle and a set of E and F pieces that were cut from a fabric different than the D rectangle. Sew the E rectangles to the long edges of the D rectangle. Sew the F rectangles to the short sides of the D/E unit. Repeat to make a total of 18 units.

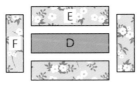 

Unit B.
Make 18.

3. To make the C units, select a G square, a set of H and I pieces, and a set of J and K pieces. Make sure all three fabrics are different. Repeat step 1 to sew the H and I pieces to the G square. Add the J pieces to the sides of the unit, and then join the K pieces to the top and bottom. Repeat to make a total of 18 units.

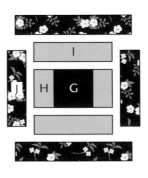 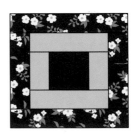

Unit C.
Make 18.

4. To make the D units, select an L rectangle, a set of M and N pieces, and a set of O and P pieces. Make sure all three fabrics are different. Repeat step 2 to sew the M and N pieces to the L rectangles. Add the O pieces to the top and bottom of the unit, and then join the P pieces to the sides. Repeat to make a total of 4 units.

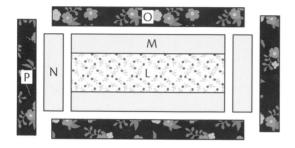

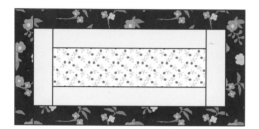

Unit D.
Make 4.

ASSEMBLING THE QUILT TOP

1. Arrange the units as shown to make one quadrant of the quilt top. Sew the units into sections, and then sew the sections together. Repeat to make a total of four quadrants, referring to the quilt assembly diagram on page 41 and the photo on page 37 to rotate the text block so it is oriented in the correct direction on the finished quilt. Each quadrant is the same, but the text must be rotated to be readable.

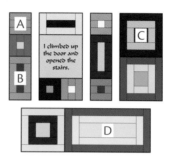

Make 1.   Make 1.

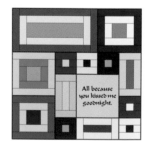

Make 1.   Make 1.

2. Join the remaining units to make two rows for the top and bottom of the quilt.

Make 2.

3. Refer to the quilt assembly diagram to sew the quadrants into two rows of two quadrants each. Make sure the text square is in the proper position so the verse reads correctly. Sew the quadrants together. Add the unit rows from step 2 to the top and bottom of the quadrants.

4. Refer to "Borders with Butted Corners" on page 44 to add the border strips to the quilt top.

Quilt assembly

FINISHING

1. Layer the quilt top with batting and backing; baste.
2. Quilt as desired.

3. Sew the binding strips together end to end using diagonal seams to make one long strip that is approximately 330" long. Refer to "Making Painless Mitered Binding" on page 45 to bind the quilt with the pieced strip.

Enlarge patterns 250%.

I climbed up the door and opened the stairs,

I said my pajamas and put on my prayers,

I turned off the bed and crawled into the light,

All because you kissed me goodnight.

GENERAL INSTRUCTIONS

THE FOLLOWING SECTION OFFERS HELPFUL HINTS FOR TECHNIQUES USED THROUGHOUT THIS BOOK, INCLUDING HOW TO FINISH THE EDGES OF YOUR QUILT WITH MY PREFERRED BINDING TECHNIQUE.

TESTING FOR ACCURATE SEAM ALLOWANCES

We all think our own ¼"-wide seam allowance is accurate, but the only way to know for sure is to test it. Sew three 1½" x 6" strips of scrap fabric together along the long edges using a ¼" seam allowance. Measure the finished width of the center strip. If it is precisely 1", you passed the test. If not, make the necessary adjustments and repeat until you get the right width.

MAKING AND USING TEMPLATES

Several of the projects in this book are made with the aid of templates. For accuracy and ease, I use premade acrylic templates whenever possible (see "Resources" on page 47 to order acrylic templates for some of the quilts in this book). You can also make your own from a wide variety of suitable materials like template plastic, cereal-box cardboard, plastic from recycled margarine tubs, etc.

To make your own templates, simply trace the pattern onto your template-making material and cut it out (don't cut the patterns from this book!). Or, if your material is not transparent, trace or photocopy the pattern onto a piece of paper, glue the pattern to your template-making material, and then cut it out. Transfer all markings from the original pattern onto the template.

To cut out the template shapes, position the template onto your fabric and use a rotary cutter to cut around it; a 28 mm or 18 mm blade works better to cut around curves. Be sure to keep your fingertips at a safe distance.

ROTARY CUTTING

With the exception of pieces cut with templates, all other pieces are cut using rotary-cutting techniques. You will need a rotary cutter, mat, and ruler. For most situations, a 24" x 16" mat and a 45 mm cutter are good all-purpose choices. My preferred ruler is the All-in-One Ruler. This is an all-purpose, comprehensive ruler, designed for quiltmakers of all skill levels. You can cut the most commonly used quilting shapes with it, including strips, squares, and half-square and quarter-square triangles. It is also extremely versatile, because it incorporates several specialty functions, such as a point trimmer, into one handy tool (see "Resources" on page 47 for ordering information).

ADDING BORDERS

There are two types of borders used for the quilts in this book: borders with butted corners and borders with mitered corners.

Borders with Butted Corners

These are the easiest borders to attach. In most instances, the side borders are sewn on first, and then the top and bottom borders are attached.

1. Measure the length of the quilt top through the center and cut two strips from the border fabric to the length required, piecing strips if necessary to achieve the required length.

2. Mark the centers of the border strips and the quilt top. Pin the borders to the sides of the quilt, matching centers and ends and easing the strips to fit if necessary. Sew the borders in place. Press the seam allowances toward the borders.

3. Measure the width of the quilt top through the center, including the side borders. Cut two strips from the border fabric to the length required, piecing strips if necessary. Mark the centers of the border strips and quilt top; then pin and sew in the same manner as the side borders, easing the strips to fit as necessary. Press the seam allowances toward the borders.

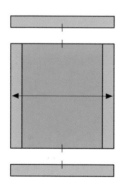

Borders with Mitered Corners

Strips for mitered borders are cut longer so there will be enough length to make the diagonal seam that joins adjacent borders.

1. Determine the finished length and width of your quilt, including borders. Make a note of these measurements for use in step 2. Add two times the width of the border plus 5" to these measurements. From the border fabric, cut two strips to the determined length and two strips to the determined width.

2. Mark the centers of the border strips and each edge of the quilt top. Mark the quilt top ¼" from each corner.

3. Using the finished quilt length measurement from step 1, measure from the center point and place a pin at each end of the side border strips to mark the length of the quilt top. Repeat with the top and bottom border strips using the finished width measurement from step 1.

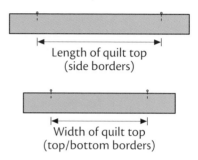

Length of quilt top
(side borders)

Width of quilt top
(top/bottom borders)

4. Pin the side borders to the quilt top, matching centers. Align the pins on the border strip with the corner marks on the quilt. Stitch the strips in place, beginning and ending at the pin marks. Repeat with the top and bottom borders.

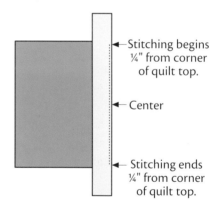

Stitching begins ¼" from corner of quilt top.

Center

Stitching ends ¼" from corner of quilt top.

5. Lay the first corner to be mitered on the ironing board. Fold under one border at a 45° angle to the other. Press and pin.

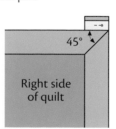

45°

Right side of quilt

6. Fold the quilt right sides together, lining up the edge of the adjacent border strips. Stitch on the pressed crease line, sewing from the corner to the outside edges.

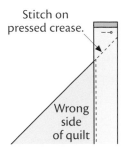

7. Trim the seam allowances to ¼". Press the seam allowances open.

8. Repeat steps 5–7 with the remaining corners.

MAKING PAINLESS MITERED BINDING

The binding technique presented here yields great-looking corners and eliminates the need to close up the edge of the binding with a pesky mitered seam. It works well with binding of any width. You do not need to make any adjustments when sewing; just cut the binding strips wider. To make this technique even easier, I've developed a tool called The Quilter's Boot which will help you miter the corners of your binding for perfect corners every time, and it can be used for three different angles. It also includes a triangle trimmer which increases patchwork accuracy. (See "Resources" on page 47.) Alternative instructions for binding your quilt using my method without the tool are also given here.

1. Place a chalk or pencil mark ¼" from each corner of the quilt top. Measure the quilt top between the marks and note these measurements; they will help you determine the length of the binding strips you need to make.

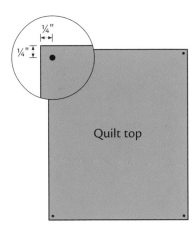

2. Cut strips of binding fabric as instructed for the project. For each edge of the quilt, you will need one strip that is approximately 6" longer than the edge to be bound. Using diagonal seams, join strips, if necessary, to make a long-enough strip.

3. Press the strips in half lengthwise, wrong sides together. With raw edges even, sew the appropriate folded strip to one edge of the quilt top, leaving approximately 3" of binding extending beyond each end. Begin sewing at the first chalk mark; stop sewing at the second chalk mark. Backstitch to secure the ends of the strip. Repeat to sew a strip to each side of the quilt.

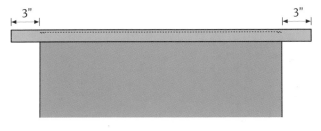

4. Place the quilt top on a flat surface with the raw edge of one binding strip facing you. Bring the folded edge toward you, stopping at the line of stitching; crease. Open up the binding and lay it flat again.

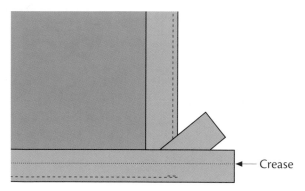

← Crease

Alternative to the All-in-One Ruler

If you do not have an All-in-One Ruler, you can make a "miter-marking guide" by drawing a diagonal line from corner to corner on a 3"-square of self-stick notepaper. Make seven or eight pencil marks at 3" intervals along two adjacent edges. Using this marking guide as a substitute for the ruler, position the guide as explained above and proceed as follows.

5. Place the All-in-One Ruler on the binding strip, aligning the diagonal dashed line of the ruler on top of the crease mark on the binding. Position the ruler so that one of the 3" marks meets the folded edge of the binding, while another 3" mark meets the backstitch. There should be an equal number of marks from the tip of the ruler to the folded edge of the binding and from the tip of the ruler to the backstitch.

6. Using a pencil or chalk marker, trace around the tip of the ruler (or marking guide), drawing a line from the folded edge of the binding to the backstitch. (Make sure the drawn line points *away* from the quilt.) Remove the ruler or guide. With the right side of the quilt facing up, fold the quilt diagonally from the corner so that the marked binding strip and the adjacent binding strip are aligned along the folded edges. Pin the binding strips together.

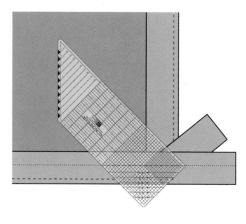

7. Sew along the marked line, starting at the folded edge and sewing to within one stitch of the tip. Stop, pivot, and take one stitch across the tip. Pivot again and continue stitching down the marked line to the backstitch. Trim ¼" away from the stitching line and turn the corner to the right side.

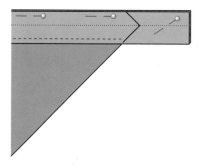

8. Repeat steps 4–7 for the remaining corners.

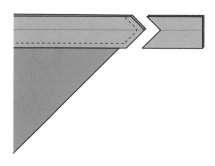

ABOUT THE AUTHOR

Cathy Wierzbicki is an experienced quiltmaker, "sew-ist," and all-around crafty person. She lives in the Pacific Northwest with her husband, Tom, but she never turns down an opportunity to be in the Midwest, where you can often find her enjoying time with her two children and three grandchildren. She looks forward to more opportunities to travel and share her love of quilting with quilters wherever they gather. Cathy has written five quilting books and countless patterns. This is her third book with Martingale & Company.

There's More Online!
See Cathy's patterns at www.timetoquilt.com. Learn more about Cathy's books at www. martingale-pub.com.

RESOURCES

ASK FOR THESE PRODUCTS AT YOUR LOCAL QUILT SHOP. IF THEY'RE NOT AVAILABLE, CONTACT THE RESOURCE LISTED.

All-in-One Ruler
Martingale & Company
20205 144th Avenue NE
Woodinville, WA 98072-8478
800-426-3126
www.martingale-pub.com

Acrylic Templates, Quilter's Boot, and
All-in-One Ruler
Time to Quilt
Cathy Wierzbicki
www.timetoquilt.com

Nine Patch with an Attitude and Think Inside the Box templates are available for $8, postpaid, by contacting the author through her website.

Preprinted Fabric Panels
Block Party Studios, Inc.
1503 W. K Ave.
Nevada, Iowa 50201
800-419-2812
www.blockpartystudios.com

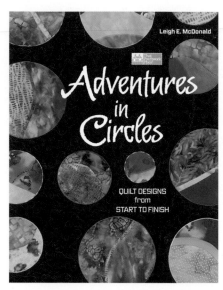
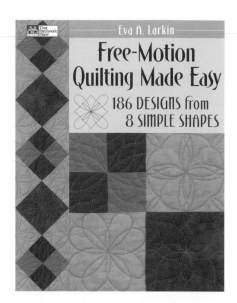
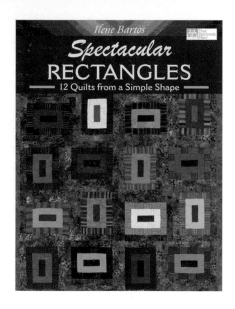